Coloring book for adults and kids amazing cactus flower image for design

This coloring book is belongs to

....

....

....

Cactus
is my love

CACTI TOCACTI YOU

Cactus

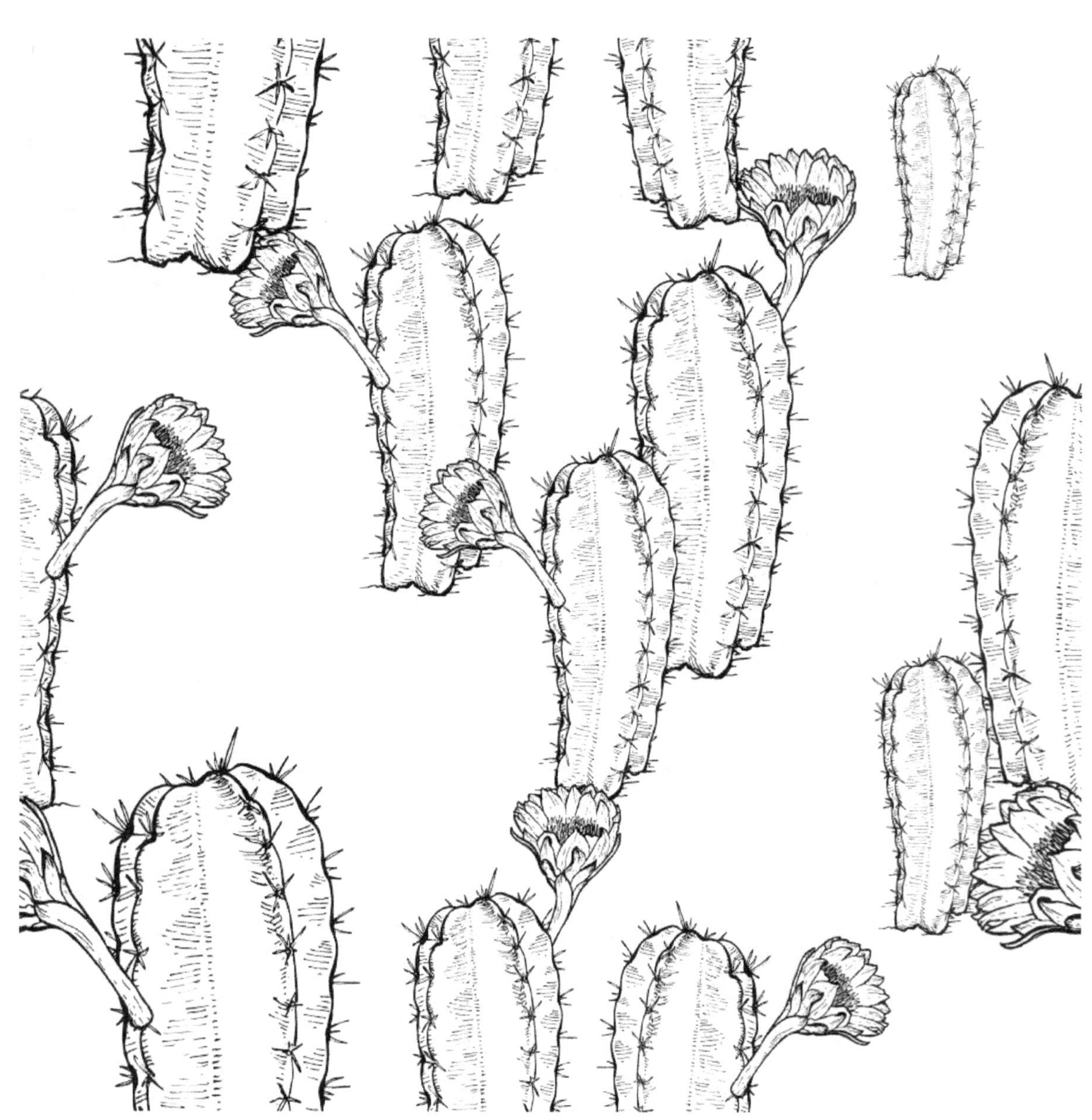

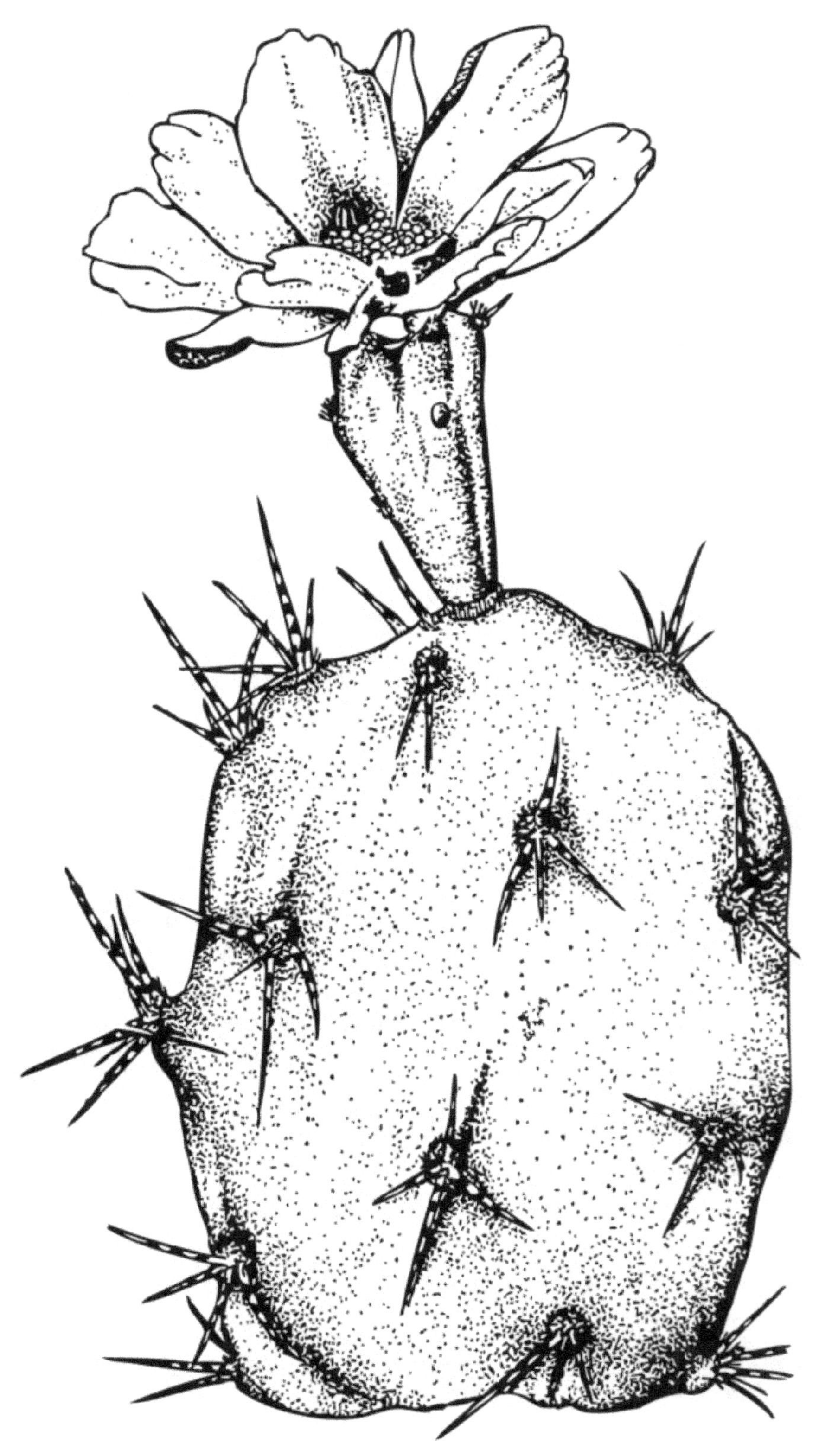

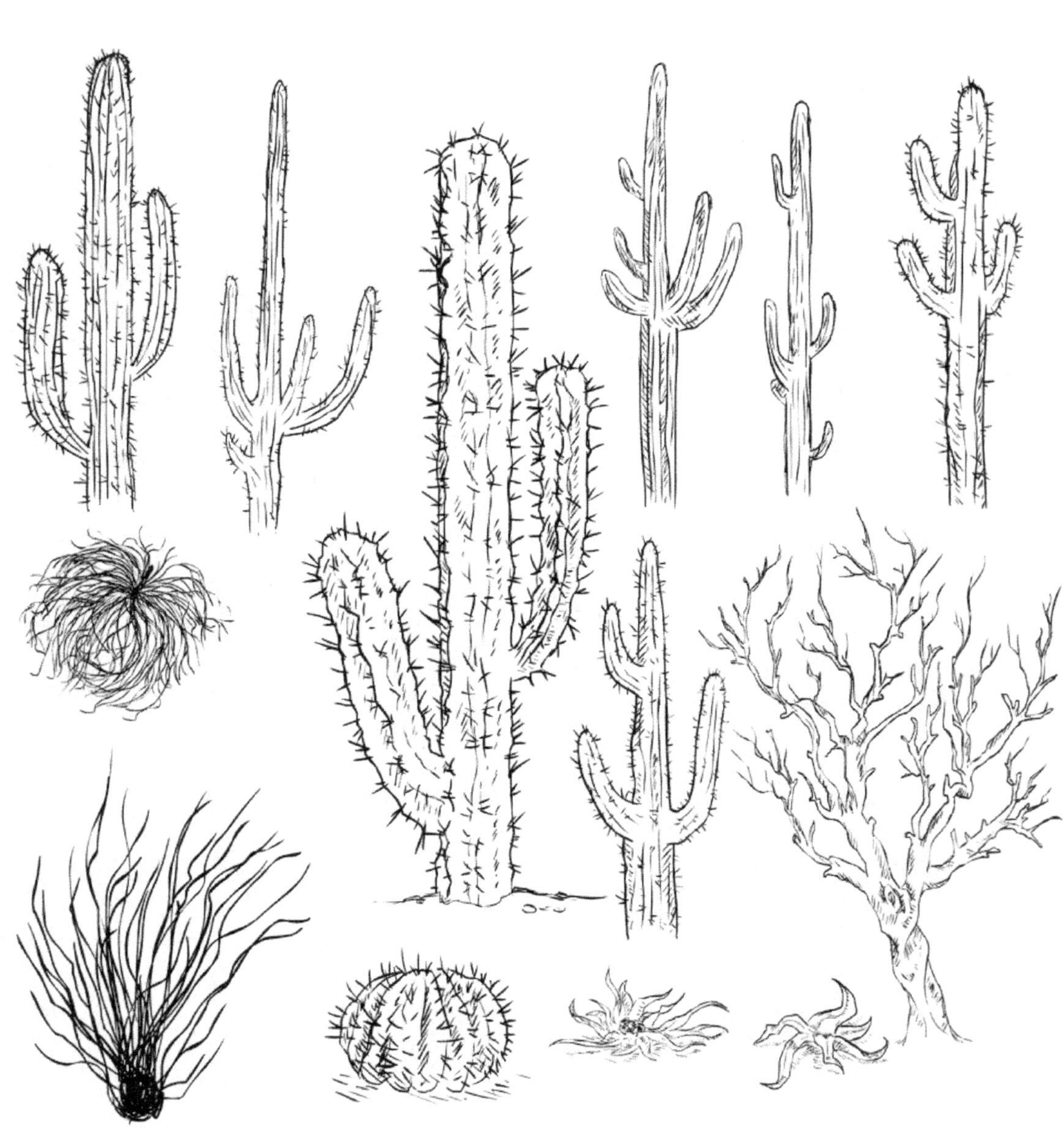

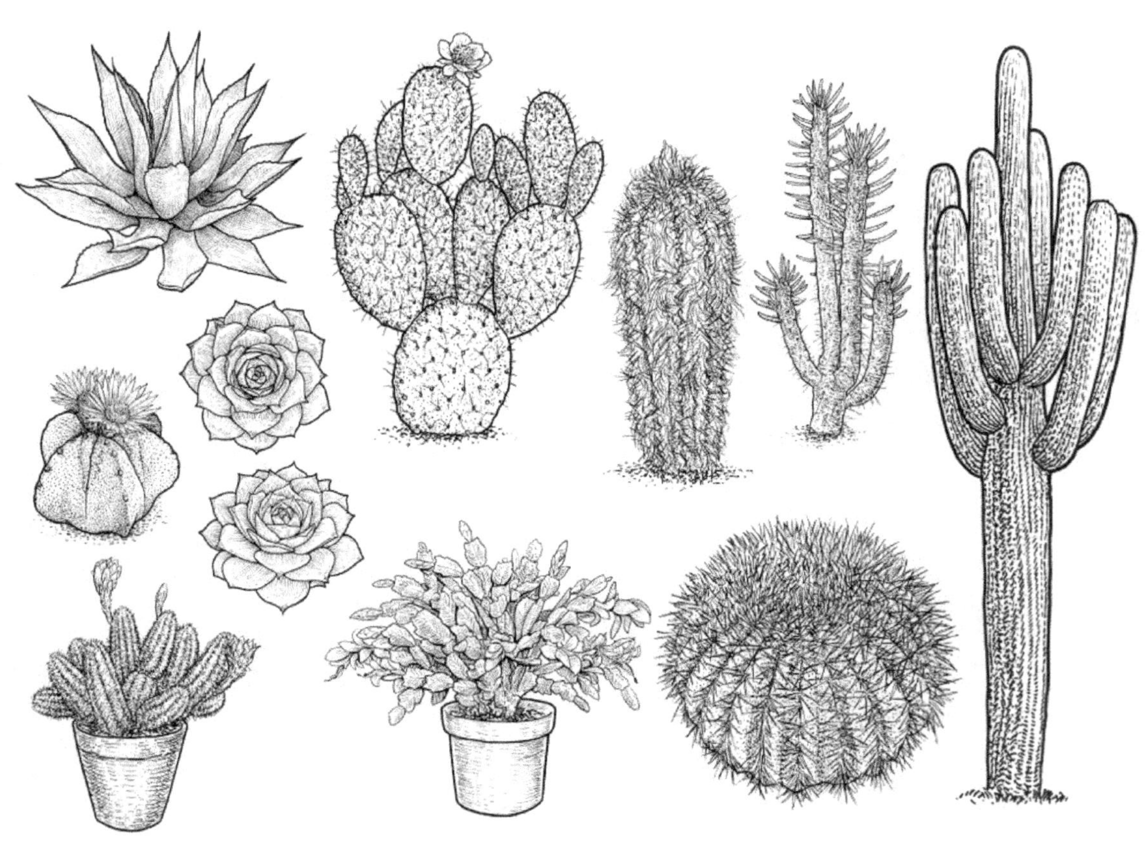

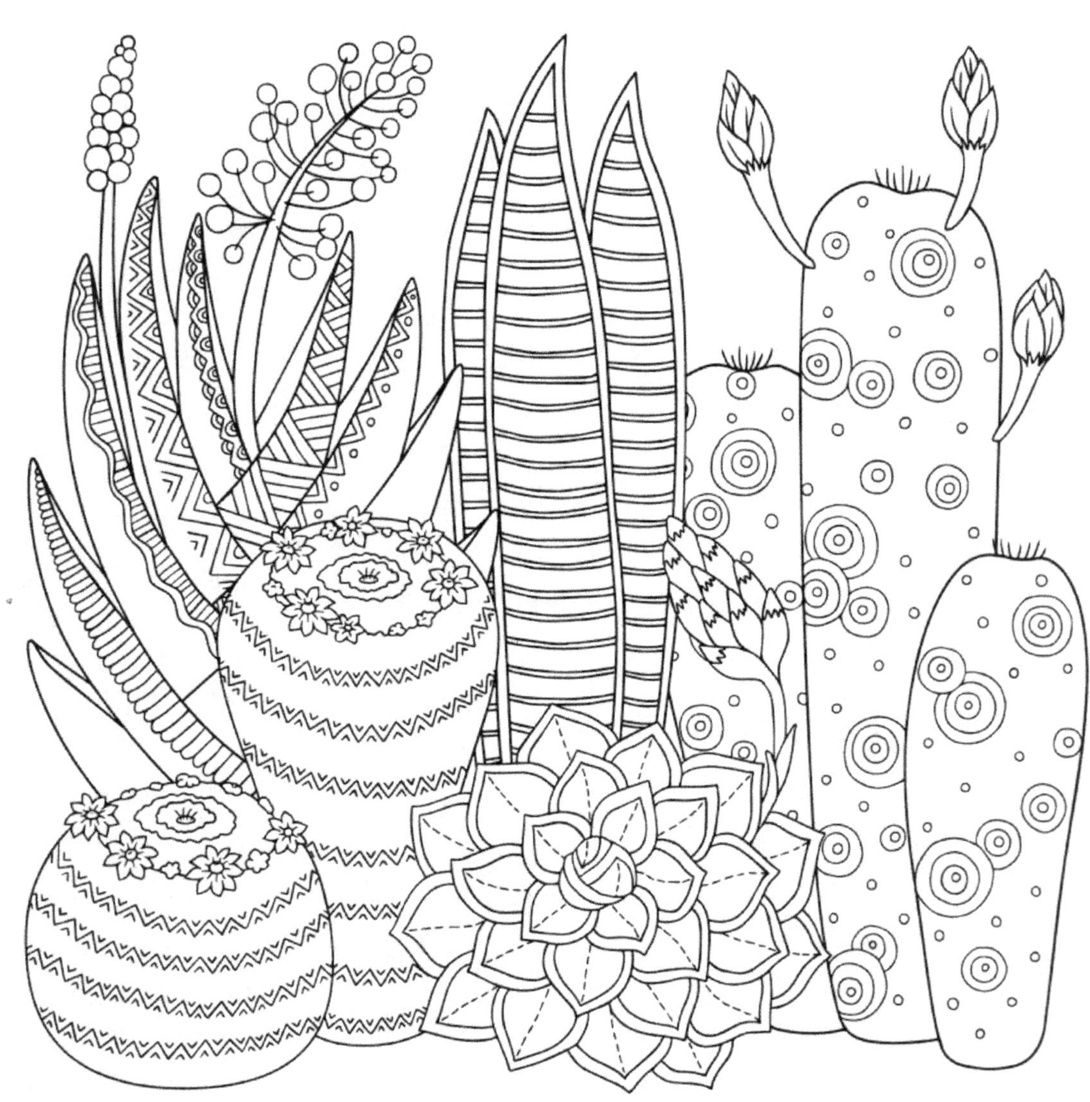

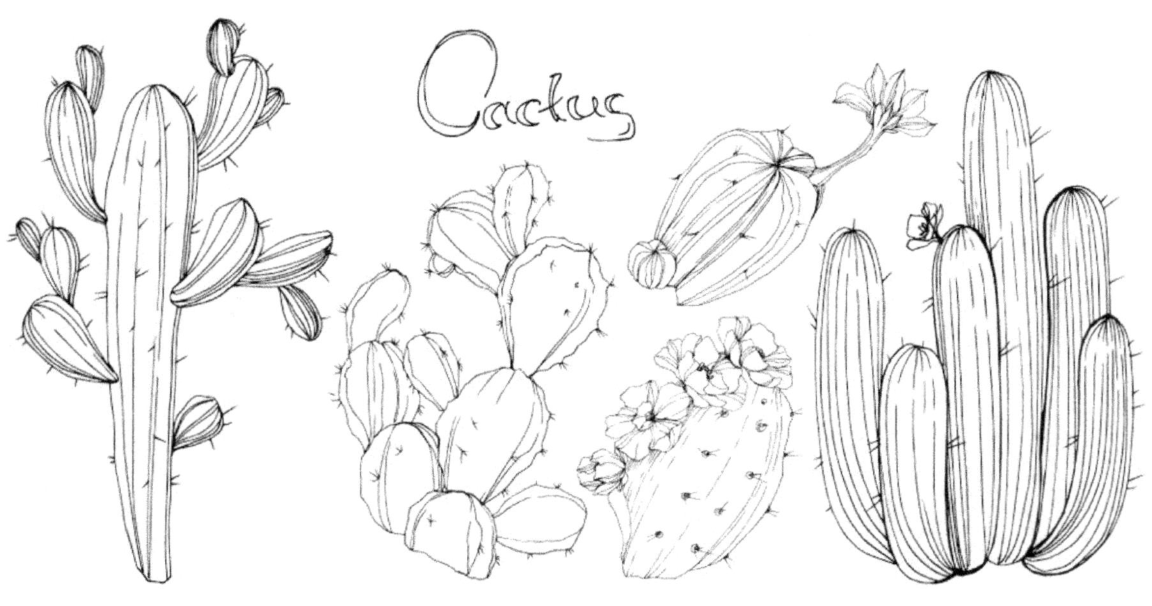

Cactus

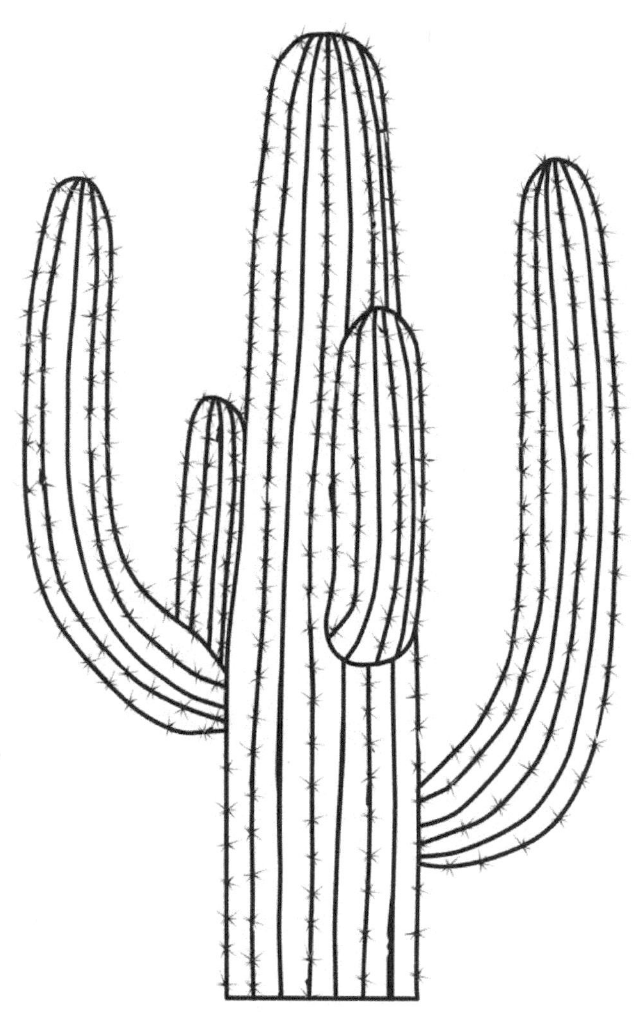

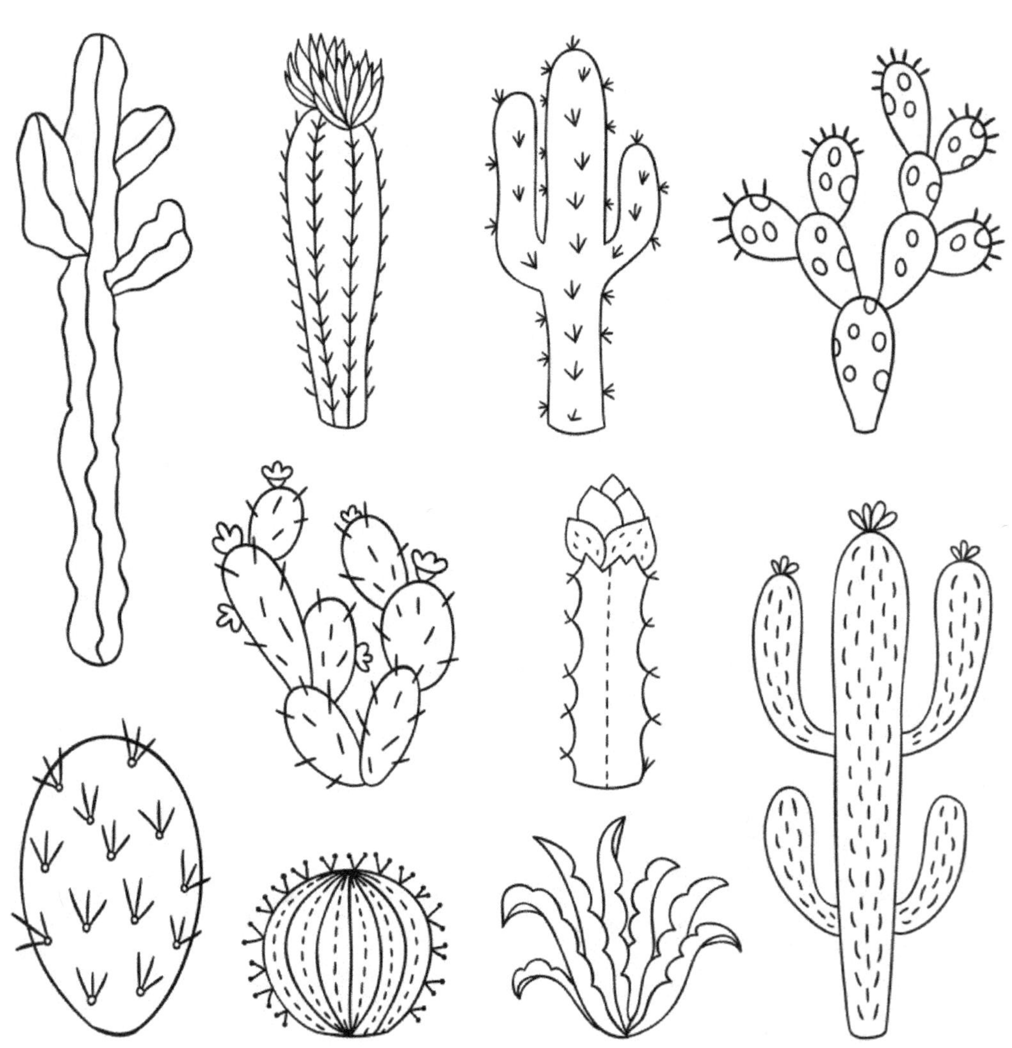

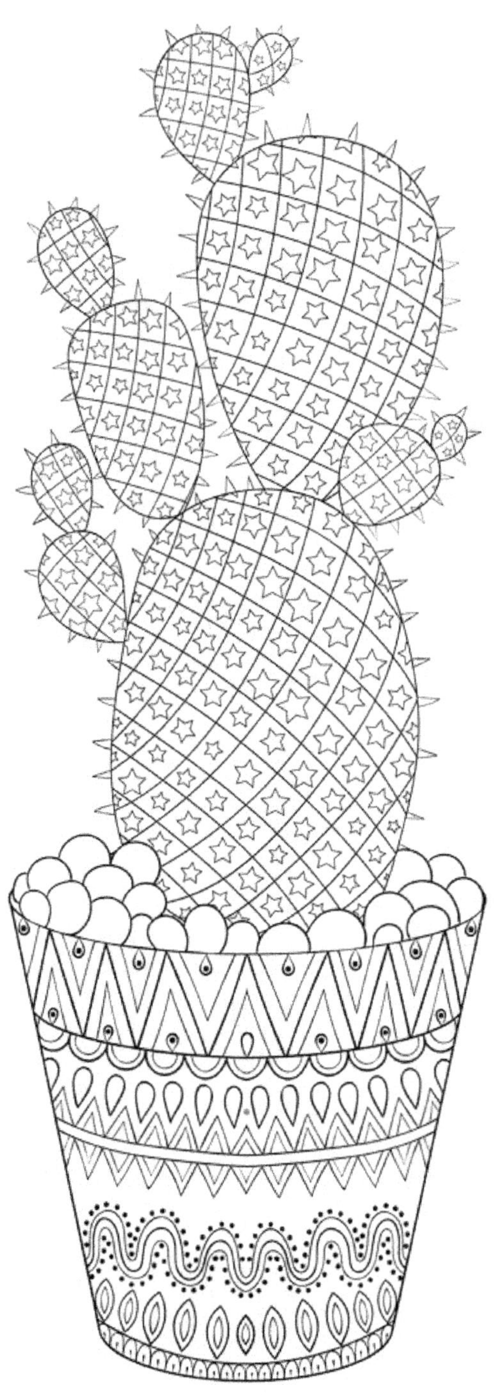

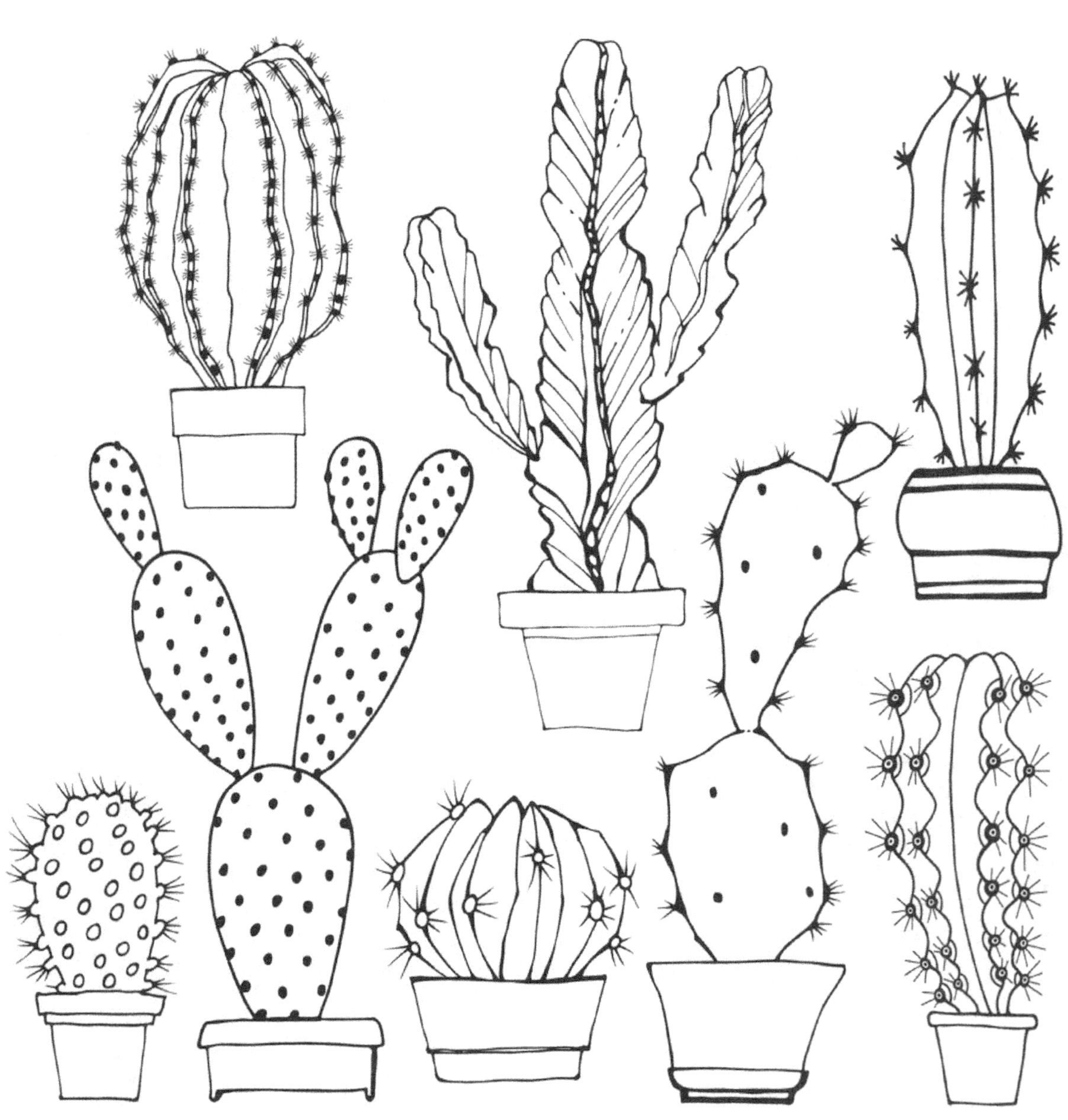

www.ingramcontent.com/pod-product-compliance
Lightning Source LLC
Chambersburg PA
CBHW080037260726
48658CB00007B/2651